MW01489279

AVA GALA

The Ultimate Guide to Birthday Party Planning For Beginners

From vision to celebration, a step by step guide for crafting perfect parties, that are memorable and stay in budget, even if you've never done it before.

First published by 9 Six 8 Media 2024

Copyright © 2024 by Ava Gala

All rights reserved. No part of this publication may be reproduced, stored or transmitted in any form or by any means, electronic, mechanical, photocopying, recording, scanning, or otherwise without written permission from the publisher. It is illegal to copy this book, post it to a website, or distribute it by any other means without permission.

First edition

This book was professionally typeset on Reedsy.
Find out more at reedsy.com

To Nadia. May your 30th be your first and best party ever!
And for you, for keeping the joy of life alive by celebrating yourself and others.

Contents

Prologue

Many of us take for granted the ability to have yearly celebrations marking the milestones in our lives great and small. We often forget that celebrating our birthday is a privilege. I hope this book serves those who have never felt the joy of a gathering meant solely to celebrate them, and the life they are living.

Introduction

Celebrating a birthday is more than marking another year; it's a joyous occasion to honor life, create memories, and bring together those we cherish. Whether it's a milestone birthday or a simple gathering, each celebration is a testament to individuality and the joy that person brings into the lives of others. Being able to celebrate another birthday, milestone or not, is a privilege that we should not take for granted. However, planning the perfect birthday party can feel daunting, especially if you didn't grow up in a community that celebrated birthdays or hosted many gatherings. From selecting a theme to managing the guest list, each detail plays a crucial role in bringing the day to life.

"The Ultimate Birthday Party Planning Guide" is your comprehensive companion through the exciting journey of organizing a birthday celebration. Crafted with love and attention to detail, this guide aims to simplify the planning process, ensuring you can focus on what truly matters—celebrating the special day with friends and family. Whether you're planning a cozy home party or an extravagant bash, this guide will provide you with creative ideas, practical advice, and step-by-step instructions to ensure your party is a hit.

We'll navigate through setting the stage with the perfect theme, crafting a budget that works for you, and choosing a venue that sets the tone for your celebration. We've got you covered from sending out eye-catching invitations to selecting the right menu and entertainment options. Plus, we'll share tips on capturing those precious memories, ensuring the joy and laughter of the day are preserved forever.

With this guide in hand, you'll be empowered to plan a birthday party that reflects the unique spirit of the honoree, creating a day filled with joy, laughter, and unforgettable memories. So let's turn the page and start this exciting journey together, creating a celebration that will be talked about for years to come.

1

Setting the Stage

Determining the Party Theme

The theme of a birthday party sets the tone for the entire celebration, guiding choices in everything from decorations to invitations, and even the menu. A well-chosen theme can transform a simple celebration into an immersive experience for the guest of honor and attendees alike. Here's how to pinpoint the perfect theme for your upcoming birthday bash.

Start with the star of the show: the birthday person. Consider their interests, hobbies, and dreams. Is there a particular movie, era, or activity they adore? The theme should reflect what they love, ensuring the party feels personal and special. For children, favorite cartoons or fairy tales are popular options, while adults might appreciate themes related to their hobbies, favorite travel destinations, a cherished decade, or even something as simple as a favorite color.

The time of year can also inspire your theme choice. A summer party might lend itself well to a tropical or beach theme, while a winter celebration could embrace a cozy, winter wonderland concept. Seasonal themes can also help in deciding on indoor vs. outdoor settings, potentially impacting your venue choice.

Don't be afraid to think outside the box. Hybrid themes, such as "Jungle Cats at the Oscars" or "Superheroes at the Beach," can offer a unique twist and make the party memorable. Flexibility is key; the theme should be broad enough to allow for creative interpretations in decorations, activities, and food, ensuring the planning process remains fun rather than becoming a source of stress.

If coming up with a theme seems stressful and you feel like you have to get wildly creative take a breath! Themes can be as simple as "

Things to consider

The Guest List

Selecting a theme that is age-appropriate and engaging for the majority of your guests will enhance the overall enjoyment and participation in the party.

Scalability and Budget

Themes vary in execution from lavish to budget-friendly, yet their value truly lies in the creativity and thoughtfulness behind the execution, not the cost. Choose one that aligns with your budget constraints

Full Integration

Envision how it will play out across different aspects of the party ie: potential activities, decorations, and menu items that align with the theme.

If you find yourself excited by the possibilities and can envision a cohesive celebration, you've likely found your perfect theme.

Remember, the most important outcome is that the theme brings joy and excitement to the birthday person, making their special day unforgettable.

Deciding on the Date, Time, and Duration

After establishing the party's theme, the next critical step in the planning process is to decide on the date, time, and overall duration of the event. These elements are key to ensuring maximum attendance and enjoyment. Here's how to navigate these decisions:

Setting the Date & Time

Consider the Birthday Person: Always aim for the party to be as close to the birthday person's actual birth date as possible, but flexibility is essential.

Check with VIP Guests

Before finalizing the date, reach out to close family and friends who must be at the party. Their availability can help narrow down the options.

Be Mindful of Holidays and Special Events

Avoid planning the party on or near major holidays or events that might conflict with guests' availability. Additionally, any local events that could affect travel or venue availability.

Age Consideration

Early afternoons are perfect for young children, who may have early bedtimes, while evening parties might be more suitable for adults.

Type of Party

The nature of the celebration can also dictate the best time. For example, a brunch theme fits naturally in the late morning, whereas a dinner party is best suited for the evening.

Duration Expectations

Factor in traditional meal times if you plan to serve food. Guests will have expectations based on the time of day (e.g., lunch, dinner, or light snacks).

Age Appropriateness

Younger children's parties often run shorter, typically 2-3 hours, as their attention spans and energy levels wane more quickly. Adult gatherings, on the other hand, may last longer, especially if they're more social or include a meal.

Activities and Program

Map out the planned activities to get a sense of how much time you'll need. Include buffer time for transitions between activities, meals, and any spontaneous fun.

Venue Restrictions

If you're hosting the party at an external venue, be aware of any time restrictions they might have. These can limit your party duration and should be incorporated into your planning.

Once you've decided on the date, time, and event duration, communicate these details clearly in your invitations. Provide a start and end time to set expectations for guests, and if there are any specific activities planned (e.g., a magic show, or cake cutting), you might hint at these timings to ensure guests don't miss out on key moments.

It's also wise to have some flexibility and a backup plan, especially if you're having an outdoor party. Weather can be unpredictable, so consider what your options are in case of inclement weather or other unforeseen changes.

Guest List Creation: Considerations and Etiquette

The creation of a guest list is a pivotal step in party planning that directly influences the atmosphere, dynamics, and logistics of the event. Thoughtful consideration and adherence to etiquette can make this process smoother and ensure the celebration feels inclusive, joyful, and well-organized.

Considerations for Crafting Your Guest List

Budget and Venue Constraints

The size of your guest list is often dictated by your budget and the capacity of your chosen venue. More guests mean higher costs and space requirements, so start by understanding these limits.

The Birthday Person's Wishes

Center the preferences of the honoree—after all, the day is about them. Ensure that key friends and family members are included on the list. For children's parties, consider whether classmates or close friends should be invited.

Group Dynamics

Think about how guests will interact. A harmonious mix can enhance the enjoyment for everyone. Be mindful of inviting guests who will get along well and contribute positively to the party atmosphere.

Special Considerations for Children's Parties

Deciding whether to invite the entire class, just close friends, or a mix of school friends and relatives can be challenging. Consider the feelings of those not invited and the practicality of hosting a larger group.

Be transparent about who is invited, especially for events where plus-ones or children might be a question. This clarity can be communicated gently but directly in the invitations. For example, for adult parties, you'll have to consider if you are allowing plus ones based on the budget and venue has the space to do so. If so, include this information on the invite to avoid confusion. Be mindful of feelings among school friends or tight-knit communities. Discretion and tact in how invitations are distributed can prevent hurt feelings.

For example, **do not hand out invitations in a group where everyone in the group is not invited.** Same thing for inviting school or work friends, do not pass out invitations in a classroom/office, etc... where everyone is not invited.

Although it seems obvious, this happens more often than you'd believe.

Your choice of invitation can also reflect the nature of your guest list. Digital invites might be more suitable for a casual, informal gathering, while printed invitations can add a touch of formality and tradition.

Finally, clearly state the need for RSVPs by a specific date to manage your guest list effectively. This assists with final preparations and ensures no guest is overlooked.

Handling Special Requests and Changes

Things always come up last minute or there are details that you may have overlooked. Here are a few examples.

Dietary Restrictions and Allergies

Ask guests to inform you of any special dietary needs or allergies well in advance. This shows consideration for their comfort and safety.

Last-Minute Additions or Cancellations

Be prepared to gracefully handle adjustments to the guest list, including accommodating last-minute guests if possible and understanding cancellations.

2

Establishing a Realistic Budget

Budget Planning

Creating a budget for a birthday party is the cornerstone of event planning. It's the road map that guides your decisions and ensures you can celebrate without financial stress. Establishing a realistic budget means balancing your vision with what you can afford, allowing you to prioritize the elements most important to you and your guest of honor.

Here's how to approach it:

Step 1: Determine Your Total Budget

Start by deciding the total amount you're willing to spend on the party. Consider all sources of funding, whether it's savings specifically set aside for this occasion, contributions from family members, or other means. This total will be your guiding light as you allocate funds to different aspects of the event.

Step 2: List All Potential Expenses

Break down the party into all possible expenses to ensure no detail is overlooked. Common categories include:

- Venue rental
- Food and beverages
- Decorations
- Entertainment
- Invitations
- Party favors
- Photography
- Cake
- Gifts for the birthday person

Step 3: Prioritize Spending

With your list in hand, prioritize these expenses based on their importance to the birthday person's experience and the overall party vibe you aim to create. For instance, if the guest of honor values a great meal over elaborate decorations, allocate more of your budget to catering..

Step 4: Shop Around for Quotes

Before finalizing any part of your budget, gather quotes from multiple vendors for services and supplies. This research can help you identify where you might save money or where you may need to increase your budget to meet your expectations.

Step 5: Keep a Contingency Fund

Unexpected expenses can and do arise. Set aside a portion of your budget (typically 10-15%) as a contingency fund. This safety net ensures you can handle surprises without derailing your financial plan.

Step 6: Track Your Spending

As you start booking vendors and purchasing items, keep meticulous records of your expenditures. Compare these against your initial budget regularly to ensure you're on track. This vigilance helps prevent overspending and allows you to adjust allocations as needed.

Budget-Saving Tips

- DIY Where Possible: Leveraging your creative skills for decorations, invitations, or even the cake can significantly reduce costs.
- Leverage Connections: Borrow items from friends or family, like party games or serving dishes, to avoid unnecessary rentals or purchases.
- Opt for Digital Invitations: Save on printing and postage by using digital platforms to send out invitations.
- Choose Off-Peak Times: Hosting your party during off-peak times can save on venue and service costs.
- Limit the Guest List: While it may be difficult, keeping the guest list in check is one of the most effective ways to manage your budget.

Remember, the goal of your budget is not to limit the fun but to ensure that fun happens within a framework that doesn't lead to financial strain. With careful planning and a bit of creativity, you can host a memorable birthday party that celebrates the guest of honor in style—without breaking the bank.

Tips for Cost-Saving Without Compromising Quality

Planning a birthday party with a keen eye on the budget doesn't mean you have to skimp on quality. There are numerous strategies to stretch your dollar further, ensuring the celebration feels generous and joyful without overspending. Here are some tips to help you save costs while maintaining the sparkle of your event:

Leverage Bulk Buying

For items like decorations, party favors, or even non-perishable food items, buying in bulk can offer significant savings. Wholesale stores and online bulk suppliers are great resources. Not only does this approach reduce costs, but it also ensures you have plenty of supplies on hand.

Opt for Versatile Decor

Choose decorations that offer the biggest impact for the least amount of money and can be used in various ways. For example, string lights and tulle can be used to create a magical ambiance, whether indoors or out, and can be reused for future events.

Get Creative with Food and Drink

Catering can be one of the most significant expenses in party planning. Consider these alternatives:

- Potluck Style: Encourage guests to bring a dish to share. This approach not only cuts down on costs but also adds variety to the menu.
- Homemade Over Store-bought: Home-prepared foods and snacks are often cheaper and more personal than catered options. Simple, elegant appetizers or a homemade cake can be very special.
- Signature Drink: Instead of a full bar, offer a signature drink that fits the party theme. This can be a fun and cost-effective way to serve beverages.

DIY Where Feasible

From invitations to decorations to entertainment, there's a DIY option for almost every aspect of party planning. Utilize online tutorials and resources to create professional-looking items at a fraction of the cost. This approach also adds a personal touch to the celebration.

Use Digital Platforms

Digital invitations and thank you notes are not only eco-friendly but also free or very low cost. Platforms like Evite or Canva offer a range of customizable options that look great and save on printing and postage.

Choose Off-Peak Times and Days

Saturdays are prime time for parties, which means venues and services often charge a premium. Consider hosting your party on a Sunday or a weekday for potentially lower rates, or choose a morning time slot which can also be cheaper and less sought-after.

Simplify the Venue

Sometimes the best venue is a free one. Parks, backyards, or community centers can offer the perfect backdrop for your party at little to no cost. With the right decorations and setup, these spaces can be transformed into something truly special.

Borrow Instead of Buy

Before purchasing new items for the party, see if you can borrow what you need from friends or family. This could include party games, serving dishes, or even decorations. It saves money and supports a spirit of community and sharing.

Negotiate with Vendors

Don't accept the first price quoted by vendors. Whether it's for the venue, entertainment, or food, there's often room to negotiate. Ask if there are package deals or if certain services can be adjusted to fit within your budget.

Focus on Meaningful Activities

Instead of hiring expensive entertainers, think about what the birthday person loves and plan activities around those interests. Games, crafts, or a movie marathon can be just as memorable and far more personal.

By implementing these cost-saving tips, you can organize a birthday party that feels thoughtful and abundant without an extravagant price tag. The key is to focus on the elements that truly matter to the guest of honor, making smart choices that align with those priorities. With creativity and planning, it's entirely possible to celebrate in style while keeping your budget intact.

Allocating Funds: Essentials vs. Extras

When planning a birthday party on a budget, understanding how to allocate your funds between essential elements and delightful extras can make all the difference. Essentials are the non-negotiables that form the backbone of the party, while extras are the special touches that can enhance the celebration. Here's how to strike the perfect balance:

Essentials: The Non-Negotiables

- Venue: Whether it's a home party or a rented space, ensuring you have a suitable location is paramount. Consider free or low-cost options like community centers, parks, or a friend's backyard to keep costs down.
- Food and Beverages: Providing guests with refreshments is a must. Focus on crowd-pleasers that are easy to prepare and serve. Think about the time of day for the party to potentially minimize the need for a full meal.
- Basic Decorations: Decorations set the mood but don't need to break the bank. Balloons, streamers, and DIY decor can create a festive atmosphere without costing a lot.
- Activities/Entertainment: Keeping guests entertained doesn't have to be expensive. Plan a mix of free activities, like games, that align with the party theme.

Extras: The Delightful Touches

- Themed Decorations and Specialty Items: Upgrading to themed tableware or investing in a few standout decor pieces can add to the ambiance, but these items should be considered after covering the essentials.
- Professional Entertainment: Hiring a DJ, magician, or entertainer can make the party memorable but evaluate if the entertainment value justifies the cost.
- Custom Invitations: While digital invitations are cost-effective and

efficient, custom-printed invitations can add a personal touch if your budget allows.

- Party Favors: These are a "nice-to-have" and can be as simple as a small bag of themed goodies. Consider DIY options or something homemade to add a personal, cost-effective touch.

Allocating Your Budget

- List and Prioritize: Start by listing all potential expenses, then categorize them into essentials and extras. Prioritize within each category based on the guest of honor's preferences and the overall impact on the party experience.
- Research and Estimate Costs: Get a rough estimate for each item on your list. This will give you a clearer picture of where your money will go and help identify areas where you might cut back or reallocate funds.
- Allocate Funds Based on Priority: Begin by allocating funds to the essentials, ensuring the basics are covered. Whatever remains can be distributed among the extras, prioritizing those that will most enhance the guest experience.
- Track and Adjust: Keep a close eye on your spending as you book vendors and make purchases. Be prepared to adjust your allocations, perhaps sacrificing some extras if essential costs are higher than anticipated.

Maximizing the Impact of Your Budget

- Focus on Impactful Elements: Invest in elements that will have the greatest impact on your guests' experience. A well-thought-out menu or a few strategically placed decorations can have more wow factor than spreading your budget too thin across many areas.
- DIY Where Possible: Tap into your creativity to DIY elements that can save money without compromising the party's feel. Invitations, decorations, and even entertainment can often be handled in-house with a little effort and imagination.

- Borrow and Upcycle: Before purchasing new items, see if friends or family have things you can borrow. Upcycling and repurposing items can also give your party a unique and personal touch.

Understanding the balance between essentials and extras allows you to create a memorable and fun birthday party within your budget constraints. By focusing on what truly matters and making smart, informed decisions about where to spend, you can celebrate in style without financial worry.

3

Home Party vs. External Venue: Pros and Cons

Where to host the party

Deciding between hosting a birthday party at home and opting for an external venue is a pivotal choice that significantly impacts the event's atmosphere, logistics, and budget. Both options offer distinct advantages and challenges. Understanding these can help you make an informed decision that aligns with your party goals, budget, and personal preferences.

Home Party: The Comfort of Familiarity
Pros:

- Cost-Effectiveness: Generally, home parties are more budget-friendly, eliminating venue rental fees. You have more control over expenses related to food, decorations, and activities.
- Flexibility: Hosting at home offers flexibility in scheduling and duration, allowing for early setup and late teardown. It's easier to manage last-minute changes in a familiar environment.

- Personal Touch: Home parties often feel more intimate and personal. You can tailor the setup to perfectly suit the birthday person's tastes and preferences without the constraints of a venue's policies.
- Convenience: For families with young children or pets, having the party at home can be more convenient and less stressful than transporting supplies and managing logistics at an external location.

Cons:

- Space and Capacity Limitations: Homes, especially smaller ones, may restrict guest count and the scope of activities you can plan.
- Cleanup: Post-party cleanup can be daunting, with the responsibility falling entirely on the hosts.
- Potential for Damage: Hosting a large group can put your home at risk for spills, breakages, and wear.

External Venue: The Allure of Something Different
Pros:

- Space and Amenities: External venues typically offer more space and specialized amenities, such as professional sound systems, lighting, and catering services. This can elevate the event experience.
- No Cleanup Worries: Venues often include setup and cleanup in their packages, relieving you of the aftermath hassle. This means you can focus more on enjoying the party.
- Professional Management: Venue staff can handle many logistics, from parking to food service, ensuring the event runs smoothly. Their experience can also be invaluable in planning and execution.
- Unique Experience: Celebrating at a unique venue can make the birthday party memorable and special, offering experiences (like aquariums, zoos, or theme parks) that aren't possible at home.

Cons:

- Cost: Renting a venue can significantly increase the overall budget when you factor in rental fees, mandatory vendor use, and higher food and beverage costs.
- Less Flexibility: Venues often have strict scheduling windows, set up rules, and limitations on decorations or outside food, which can restrict your party planning.
- Booking Challenges: Popular venues can require booking months in advance, and you may have to work around their availability rather than your preferred date.

Making the Decision

When choosing between a home party and an external venue, consider the following:

- Budget: How much are you willing to spend? Remember to account for all potential costs associated with each option.
- Guest List Size: How many people are you planning to invite, and can your chosen location comfortably accommodate them?
- Party Theme and Activities: Does your party theme or planned activities require specific settings or equipment that one option might accommodate better than the other?
- Personal Preferences: Consider the birthday person's preferences and comfort level with hosting at home versus an external location.

Balancing the pros and cons of each option with your party vision and practical considerations will help you choose the right setting for a memorable celebration. Whether at home or an external venue, the key is to create an enjoyable experience that honors the birthday person in a setting that feels right for you and your guests.

Factors to Consider When Selecting a Venue

Choosing the right venue is crucial for the success of a birthday party. It sets the stage for the event's overall vibe, influences guest comfort, and impacts the feasibility of your planned activities. When evaluating potential venues, consider the following factors to ensure the chosen location aligns with your party goals, budget, and guest needs.

1. Size and Capacity

- Guest Fit: Ensure the venue can comfortably accommodate your guest list. Consider not just seating, but also space for activities, entertainment, and mingling.
- Flexibility: Some venues offer adjustable spaces that can be scaled to suit the size of your party, providing a cozy setting for smaller groups or ample space for larger gatherings.

2. Location

- Accessibility: The venue should be easily accessible for all guests, considering factors like distance from guests' homes, public transport links, and parking availability.
- Environment: The surrounding area should be safe and pleasant, enhancing the overall experience of your attendees.

3. Cost and Availability

- Budget Alignment: Compare venue costs against your total budget, accounting for any additional charges (e.g., service fees, setup costs).
- Date Flexibility: Popular venues book up fast, especially on weekends or during holiday seasons. Having flexible dates can increase your options.

4. Amenities and Services

- Catering: Some venues require you to use their catering services, while others may allow outside vendors. Consider this in light of your menu preferences and budget.
- Facilities: Check for essential amenities like restrooms, changing areas, and kitchen facilities. Also, assess the need for tables, chairs, and AV equipment.
- Staff Support: Determine if the venue provides staff for setup, cleanup, and technical support, as this can significantly ease the logistical burden.

5. Atmosphere and Décor

- Theme Compatibility: The venue should complement or be adaptable to your party theme. Consider how much additional decoration will be required to transform the space to your vision.
- Natural Ambience: A venue with its own character and charm can reduce the need for extensive decorations.

6. Restrictions and Policies

- Vendor Restrictions: Some venues have preferred or exclusive vendor lists, especially for catering and AV equipment. This could limit your choices and affect your budget.
- Noise Limitations: Be aware of any noise curfews or restrictions, which could impact your entertainment plans.
- Alcohol Policies: If you plan to serve alcohol, check the venue's licensing requirements and whether you need to hire a licensed bartender.

7. Weather Considerations

- Indoor vs. Outdoor: For outdoor venues, have a contingency plan in case of bad weather. Ensure there's an indoor space or adequate shelter available.
- Seasonal Factors: Choose a venue that suits the season of your party, keeping guest comfort in mind.

8. Insurance and Liability

- Protection: Some venues may require you to obtain event insurance. Understand what liabilities you and the venue hold to protect yourself in case of accidents or damage.

Making the Choice

Selecting the right venue involves weighing these factors against your personal priorities and the birthday person's preferences. A site visit is invaluable for assessing the space firsthand and imagining how your party will unfold there. Ask plenty of questions during your visit to gather all the necessary information for an informed decision.

By carefully considering each of these aspects, you can select a venue that not only fits your logistical requirements and budget but also enhances the overall experience of celebrating a special birthday.

Booking and Preparing the Venue

Securing and preparing the venue are critical steps that lay the foundation for a successful birthday party. Whether you've chosen a cozy at-home setting or an external venue, each option requires specific considerations to ensure the space is ready to welcome guests and create the desired atmosphere for the celebration. Here's a guide to navigating these processes smoothly.

Booking the Venue

Early Reservation: For external venues, it's crucial to book as early as possible, especially if the party date is during a peak season like summer or close to holidays. Start by shortlisting venues that fit your theme, budget, and size requirements, then visit them if possible to get a feel for the space and discuss your needs with the venue manager.

Understanding the Package: Clarify what is included in the venue package. Ask about decorations, catering options, entertainment facilities, and any restrictions (such as noise levels or end times). Ensure you understand the cancellation policy and any potential additional costs (e.g., overtime fees, cleaning fees).

Contract Review: Once you decide on a venue, review the contract carefully before signing. Ensure all verbal agreements are documented, and you're clear on payment schedules and what is required from both parties.

Preparing the Venue

Home Party Considerations: If you're hosting at home, start by ensuring the space is safe and accessible for all guests. Consider rearranging furniture to create more open space for activities and mingling. Decorate according to your theme, but also ensure there's a designated area for food and drinks, as well as a quiet corner for anyone who might need a break from the festivities.

External Venue Setup: Confirm the setup time with the venue. Arrive early to oversee the arrangement of tables, chairs, and decorations. Bring a checklist of all items you need to set up or deliver, such as party favors, a guest book, or special equipment for entertainment. If vendors are involved, coordinate their arrival and setup times to avoid any last-minute rush.

Decoration Strategy: Whether at home or an external venue, decorations transform the space to fit your theme. Use balloons, streamers, themed tableware, and centerpieces to create an immersive experience. Remember, less can be more—focus on key areas like the entrance, the main gathering space, and the cake table for maximum impact.

Final Walk-through: Before the guests arrive, do a final walk-through of the venue. Check that everything is in place, the bathrooms are stocked and clean, and there are no safety hazards. Ensure there's clear signage if the venue has multiple rooms or if the party is in a large outdoor space.

Emergency Preparedness: Have a first-aid kit, contact information for all vendors, and a list of guest allergies or special needs on hand. If the venue is large, designate meeting points in case someone gets lost.

Enjoy the Fruits of Your Labor: Once the party starts, take a moment to enjoy the scene you've set. Your careful planning and preparation have created the perfect backdrop for a memorable birthday celebration.

Booking and preparing the venue are tasks that require attention to detail, organization, and a touch of creativity. By following these steps, you can ensure that the chosen space not only meets your practical needs but also enhances the celebratory atmosphere of the birthday party.

4

Invitations and Guest Management

Designing and Sending Out Invitations

Invitations are more than mere notices for an event; they're the first glimpse guests have into the theme and tone of the birthday party. A well-crafted invitation not only conveys essential details but also builds anticipation and excitement. Here's how to design and dispatch invitations that charm and inform.

Understanding the Elements of an Invitation

Key Information: Ensure your invitation includes the date, time, venue address, theme (if applicable), RSVP instructions, and contact information. For children's parties, it's helpful to mention whether parents are expected to stay.

Theme Incorporation: If your party has a theme, the invitation is the perfect place to start immersing your guests in it. Use colors, fonts, and imagery that give a hint of what's to come, whether it's a sophisticated soirée or a whimsical adventure.

Choosing Your Invitation Style

Digital vs. Physical: Consider your guest list and the formality of the event when deciding between digital and physical invitations. Digital invitations are convenient and environmentally friendly, ideal for casual gatherings, and easy RSVP tracking. Physical invitations, however, add a personal and traditional touch, suitable for formal or intimate celebrations.

DIY or Professional Design: Depending on your budget and personal prefer-ence, you can either design the invitations yourself using tools like Canva or commission a professional. DIY invitations allow for a personal touch and are cost-effective, while professional designs can elevate the look of your invitations for a special touch.

Timing and Distribution

Send Early: Aim to send invitations 4-6 weeks before the event to give guests ample time to arrange their schedules. For larger or more formal parties, sending them out even earlier can be considerate.

RSVP Deadlines: Set an RSVP deadline at least two weeks before the party to finalize headcounts for catering and activities. This also allows time to follow up with guests who haven't responded.

Personalizing Invitations

Special Requests: Use invitations to communicate any special requests, such as wearing specific attire for the theme, bringing a favorite book instead of a gift, or any other participatory elements you're incorporating.

Accessibility and Inclusivity: Ensure your invitation is accessible to all guests. This includes providing clear directions, accessibility information about the venue, and contact information for any questions or accommodations needed.

Final Checks and Distribution

Proofread: Before finalizing your invitations, double-check for typos, correct date and time, and clarity of information. It can be helpful to have another person review it as well.

Distribution Method: For digital invitations, ensure you have current email addresses or phone numbers. For physical invitations, verify postal addresses. Personal delivery can also be a delightful touch for close friends and family.

Sending out invitations is a critical step in the party planning process that sets the stage for your event. By carefully considering the design, content, and timing of your invitations, you ensure that your guests are well-informed, excited, and eager to attend the celebration.

Managing RSVPs and Special Requests

Efficiently managing RSVPs and accommodating special requests are key to ensuring a smooth and inclusive birthday celebration. This process not only helps with finalizing logistical details but also demonstrates consideration for your guests' needs and preferences. Here's how to navigate these aspects gracefully.

Setting Up an RSVP System

Choose a Convenient Method: Depending on the style of your invitations, select an RSVP method that's easy for guests to use. Options include email, phone calls, text messages, or a designated event website. Digital invitations often come with built-in RSVP tracking features.

Clear Instructions: Make the RSVP process as straightforward as possible.

Clearly state where and how to RSVP, the deadline for responses, and any additional information you need from guests, such as dietary restrictions or intent to bring a plus-one.

RSVP Deadline: Set the RSVP deadline two to three weeks before the party. This timeframe allows you to follow up with non-responders and adjust plans accordingly without scrambling at the last minute.

Tracking Responses

Organize a List: Keep a centralized list or spreadsheet to track RSVPs and any special requests or needs that guests mention. Update this list regularly as responses come in, so you always have an accurate count and can adjust plans as needed.

Follow-Up Strategy: For those who haven't responded by the deadline, a polite follow-up is necessary. A friendly message or call can remind them to RSVP and express your hope that they can attend. Sometimes, guests appreciate the reminder amidst their busy schedules.

Handling Special Requests

Dietary Restrictions: Today, it's common for guests to have specific dietary needs due to allergies, religious practices, or personal choices. Collect this information through the RSVP process and work with your caterer or plan your menu to accommodate these needs as best as you can.

Accessibility Needs: Ensure all guests can enjoy the party by asking about and accommodating any accessibility needs. This may involve confirming wheelchair access, planning for sign language interpretation, or preparing quiet spaces for guests who may become overstimulated.

Other Requests: Occasionally, guests may have other types of requests, such as considerations for bringing infants or inquiries about parking. Address these individually, ensuring each guest feels heard and accommodated.

Communicating with Guests

Confirmation Messages: Once RSVPs are in, consider sending out confirmation messages or emails. This can include any last-minute details about the party, a thank-you for the RSVP, and an expression of excitement to see them.

Updates and Changes: If any details of the party change significantly after the invitations have been sent out, promptly communicate these changes to your guests. Keeping everyone informed prevents confusion and ensures a smooth experience on the day of the event.

Managing RSVPs and special requests with attentiveness and efficiency is crucial for finalizing your party preparations and ensuring all guests feel welcome and valued. By implementing a system that caters to these aspects, you contribute significantly to the overall success and enjoyment of the birthday celebration.

Communication Strategies for Updates and Reminders

Effective communication is the backbone of successful event planning, ensuring that all guests are informed of any updates and reminded of the upcoming celebration. Strategic communication not only keeps the excitement building but also minimizes the chances of confusion or miscommunication. Here are key strategies to keep your guests well-informed and engaged.

Utilizing Multiple Communication Channels

Digital Platforms: For efficiency and reach, utilize digital platforms such as email, social media event pages, or messaging apps. These platforms are convenient for sending out quick updates or reminders and allow for interactive engagement with your guests.

Personal Touch: For important updates or special reminders, consider personalized phone calls or text messages, especially to key guests or those less active on digital platforms. This approach adds a warm, personal touch and ensures the message is received.

Timing Your Communications

Initial Reminder: Send an initial reminder about a week before the event, reiterating key details such as the date, time, and location. This reminder can also include any thematic elements guests might need to prepare for, such as costume details for a themed party.

Last-Minute Reminder: A day or two before the party, send a last-minute reminder with any final details. This could include parking information, weather-related updates for outdoor events, or even just a message expressing your excitement to see them.

Managing Updates

Immediate Notification: If any significant changes occur (e.g., a change in venue, time, or date), notify guests immediately. Prompt communication is crucial to allow guests to adjust their plans.

Highlight New Information: When communicating updates, clearly highlight what has changed from the original plan. Use bold text, and bullet points, or start the message with a clear statement that there has been an update to ensure the new information stands out.

Engaging and Interactive Content

Build Anticipation: Use your communications to build anticipation for the party. Share sneak peeks of decorations, menu items, or planned activities without giving away all the surprises. This creates a buzz around the event and keeps guests looking forward to it.

Interactive Elements: Encourage engagement by asking guests to share their own preparations for the party, whether it's choosing an outfit for a themed event or a special dish they're bringing for a potluck. Interaction fosters a sense of community and excitement leading up to the event.

Confirming Attendance

RSVP Confirmation: Use your reminders as an opportunity to confirm attendance, especially if you haven't heard back from some guests. A simple request for confirmation can help you finalize numbers for catering and activities.

Leveraging Templates

Consistency and Clarity: Create templates for your reminders and updates to maintain consistency in your communication. Templates help ensure that all messages are clear, concise, and contain all necessary information.

Effective communication strategies are essential for keeping guests informed and engaged in the lead-up to the birthday party. By choosing the right channels, timing your messages carefully, and incorporating engaging content, you ensure that your guests are as excited about the celebration as you are and that they arrive well-prepared for the festivities.

5

Theme and Decoration

Selecting a Theme That Aligns with the Birthday Person's Interests

Crafting a birthday celebration that resonates with the honoree's passions and preferences can turn a simple party into an unforgettable event. The key lies in selecting a theme that mirrors the interests, hobbies, and personality of the birthday person, creating an atmosphere where they feel truly celebrated. Here's a guide to ensure the theme you choose hits the mark.

Understanding the Honoree

Interests and Hobbies: Begin with what the birthday person loves. Are they drawn to the arts, sports, technology, or perhaps a certain era or genre of music? This can be a treasure trove of thematic inspiration.

Personality Traits: Consider the individual's personality. A theme that captures their essence, whether they're adventurous, a lover of glamor, or someone who appreciates the nuances of a good book, can make the party feel deeply personal.

Recent Milestones or Achievements: For an adult, consider recent life milestones or achievements that could inspire a theme, such as a new hobby, a travel destination they loved, or a career achievement.

Involvement and Exploration

Engaging the Honoree: If the party isn't a surprise, involve them in the theme selection. Their excitement and ideas can lead to a theme that's both meaningful and fun.

Observation for Surprises: For surprise parties, gather insights through observation or by chatting with their close friends and family. Look for hints in their recent interests, social media posts, or things they've expressed a desire to try or explore.

Tailoring the Theme

Adaptability: Ensure the theme can be adapted to party planning elements like decorations, activities, and food. A good theme offers plenty of inspiration for these aspects, creating a cohesive experience.

Age Appropriateness: While aligning with interests, the theme should also be age-appropriate, offering relevant enjoyment for the birthday person and their guests.

Creativity in Execution: Think creatively about how to bring the theme to life. Beyond decorations, consider themed activities, music, and even dress codes that immerse guests in the experience.

Ensuring Flexibility

Broad Appeal: While the theme should primarily cater to the birthday person's interests, consider its overall appeal to ensure guests can also connect and engage with it.

Flexibility for Guests: If the theme involves costumes or specific attire, make sure it's broad enough to allow guests flexibility and creativity in their participation without feeling burdened by the cost or effort of finding something appropriate.

Personal Touches

Integrating Personal Stories or Elements: Infuse the theme with personal touches that tell a story or highlight unique aspects of the birthday person's life. This could include photo displays, personalized decorations, or a playlist of their favorite songs.

Selecting a theme that aligns with the birthday person's interests involves a blend of thoughtful consideration, creative planning, and a keen understanding of what makes them tick. By focusing on their passions and personality, you create not just a party, but a celebration of who they are, ensuring a memorable experience for everyone involved.

Decoration Ideas and Setup Tips

Transforming a party space to reflect your chosen theme involves creativity, planning, and a few strategic choices. Decorations are key to creating an atmosphere that immerses guests in the celebration from the moment they arrive. Here's how to approach decorating for your themed birthday party, ensuring every detail contributes to a cohesive and stunning visual experience.

Starting with a Focal Point

Create a Center piece: Choose a central area for your decoration efforts. This could be a dessert table, a photo backdrop, or a seating area. A well-decorated focal point draws guests' attention and sets the tone for the entire space.

Balancing Theme with Practicality

Thematic Consistency: Ensure all decorations align with your theme, from tablecloths and centerpieces to wall hangings and lighting. Consistency helps reinforce the theme throughout the space.

Functionality: Decorations should enhance the space without hindering functionality. Ensure walkways are clear, and essential areas like the food table and bathrooms are easily accessible.

Utilizing Lighting and Color

Mood Lighting: Lighting can dramatically alter the ambiance of a party. Use string lights, lanterns, or colored lights to match your theme and create a desired mood.

Color Scheme: Stick to a color palette that complements your theme. Consistent use of colors in decorations, tableware, and even guest attire can tie the whole event together visually.

Innovative Decoration Ideas

Thematic Tablescapes: Use your theme to inspire table settings. This could involve thematic table runners, napkin folding, or centerpieces that double as conversation starters.

Interactive Decorations: Incorporate elements that engage guests, like a photo booth with themed props or a DIY station related to your theme.

Layered Decor: Think vertically and horizontally. Hanging decorations, wall art, and floor decals can add depth and interest to your party space.

Setup and Tear down Considerations

Plan Ahead: Sketch a rough layout of your party space with decoration placements. This plan will guide your setup process and ensure you have all the necessary materials.

Safety First: Ensure decorations are securely fastened and pose no safety risks. Use non-damaging hooks for hanging items and ensure nothing obstructs exits.

Efficiency in Setup: Organize decorations by area for efficient setup. Enlist help to divide and conquer tasks, ensuring everything is ready before guests arrive.

Tear down Strategy: Have a plan for taking down decorations. This is especially important for rented spaces with limited time for cleanup or when decorations are to be saved or recycled.

Decorating for a themed birthday party is about more than just aesthetics; it's about creating an experience. Through thoughtful selection and placement of decorations, you can transport your guests into the world you've envisioned, making the birthday celebration a memorable escape for everyone involved.

DIY vs. Professional Decorators

When planning a themed birthday party, one of the significant decisions you'll face is whether to decorate the venue yourself (DIY) or hire a professional decorator. Both approaches have their merits and can significantly impact the atmosphere of the celebration. Here's a comprehensive look at the pros and cons of DIY versus professional decorators to help you make an informed choice.

DIY Decorations

Consider crafting centerpieces, banners, or thematic props. Social media and craft websites offer a plethora of ideas and tutorials.

Pros:

Personal Touch: DIY decorations allow for a highly personalized setting. They enable you to incorporate unique elements that have special meaning to the birthday person, creating an intimate and heartfelt ambiance.

Cost-Effective: Generally, opting for DIY can be more budget-friendly. It allows you to control expenses closely, choosing materials and elements that fit within your financial plan.

Family and Friends Involvement: The process of creating decorations can be a fun pre-party activity, offering an opportunity for family and friends to bond and contribute to the celebration's success.

Cons:

Time-Consuming: Crafting your decorations can be incredibly time-intensive, especially for complex designs or large venues. It requires significant planning, shopping for supplies, and actual crafting time.

Skill Level: Not everyone has a knack for arts and crafts. Without certain skills, achieving the desired look might be challenging, potentially leading to frustration or results that don't meet your expectations.

Stress and Effort: Balancing decoration efforts with other aspects of party planning can be stressful. It's a considerable commitment that can add to the overall workload of organizing the event.

Professional Decorators

Pros:

Professional Expertise: Professional decorators bring experience and skills to the table. They can transform your vision into reality, often exceeding expectations with their creativity and access to high-quality materials.

Time-Saving: Hiring a professional frees up your time to focus on other aspects of the party planning. It eliminates the stress of managing one of the event's most labor-intensive parts.

Access to Resources: Professionals often have access to a wider range of decorations, including bespoke and high-end options that might not be available to the general public. They can source materials and elements that perfectly match your theme.

Cons:

Cost: The expertise of professional decorators comes at a price. Depending on the complexity of your theme and the scale of your venue, this can be one of the more significant expenses in your party budget.

Less Personal Involvement: While professionals can execute your vision, you might feel a step removed from the creative process. For those who enjoy crafting and decorating, this might detract from the experience.

Finding the Right Fit: Not all decorators are created equal. Finding a professional who understands your vision and whom you trust to execute it can be challenging. It often requires research and consultations to find the perfect match.

Making the Decision

Consider your budget, time, personal skills, and the complexity of your desired theme. For a small, intimate gathering, a DIY approach might add a charming personal touch. However, for elaborate themes or larger venues, the expertise of a professional could be invaluable, ensuring a polished and cohesive look without the added stress on your part.

In either case, the goal is the same: to create a memorable and enjoyable atmosphere that celebrates the birthday person in style. Whether through personal crafting or professional expertise, your choice should ultimately serve the vision you have for the special day.

6

Food and Beverage

Planning the Menu: Catering vs. Homemade

The menu is a central element of any birthday celebration, directly contributing to the guests' overall experience. Deciding between catering and preparing food at home is a significant choice, influenced by factors like budget, the scale of the party, and personal preferences. Here's a comprehensive look at both options to help you craft a memorable culinary experience for the birthday party.

Catering

Pros:

Convenience: One of the most significant advantages of catering is convenience. Professional caterers handle everything from menu planning to food preparation, serving, and cleanup, allowing you to focus on other aspects of the party.

Variety and Quality: Caterers can offer a wide range of menu options, accommodating various dietary needs and preferences. They're also skilled in food presentation, adding a professional touch to the dining experience.

Scalability: Catering services are well-equipped to handle events of any size, ensuring consistent quality and service whether you're hosting a small gathering or a large celebration.

Cons:

Cost: Professional catering services can be expensive, with costs varying widely based on menu complexity, service level, and guest count. This option typically consumes a significant portion of the event budget.

Less Personal Touch: While caterers work to tailor the menu to your preferences, there may be less room for personal touches or family favorite recipes that you could easily incorporate with homemade food.

Booking and Coordination: Finding the right caterer requires research, meetings, and tastings, which can be time-consuming. You'll also need to coordinate closely with them to ensure the menu aligns with your party theme and schedule.

Homemade

Pros:

Personalization: Preparing food at home allows you to customize the menu entirely, from favorite family recipes to dishes that perfectly match the party theme. This personal touch can make the celebration feel more intimate and special.

Budget-Friendly: Homemade food is generally more cost-effective than catering. It gives you control over the ingredients and quantities, helping to keep expenses down.

Family Involvement: Cooking for the party can be a way to involve family members and friends, making the preparation process a shared experience that contributes to the anticipation and enjoyment of the event.

Cons:

Time and Effort: Cooking for a large group is time-consuming and can be stressful, especially alongside other party planning responsibilities. It requires significant effort, from planning the menu and shopping for ingredients to cooking and presentation.

Logistical Challenges: Serving homemade food involves considerations like keeping dishes at the correct temperature, setting up a serving area, and managing cleanup. For larger parties, these logistical aspects can become complex.

Scalability: There's a limit to how much food you can realistically prepare and serve, especially in a home kitchen. For larger gatherings, catering might be a more practical option to ensure everyone is well-fed.

Making the Choice

When deciding between catering and homemade food, consider factors like your budget, the size of your gathering, and your desire for personalization versus convenience. A hybrid approach might also be a solution, with some dishes catered and others homemade, balancing the benefits of both options.

Ultimately, the goal is to provide a memorable and enjoyable dining experience that complements the overall theme and atmosphere of the birthday party, whether through the professional touch of a caterer or the personal charm of homemade dishes.

Ideas for Birthday Cakes and Alternative Options

A birthday celebration wouldn't be complete without the cake, a tradition that serves as the highlight of many parties. However, modern celebrations are embracing a wide range of alternative dessert options that can cater to diverse tastes, dietary restrictions, and thematic elements. Here's a guide to selecting the perfect birthday cake or alternative, ensuring the celebratory centerpiece is as memorable as the event itself.

Traditional Birthday Cakes

Custom Designs: Work with a bakery to create a cake that fits the party theme. Custom designs can range from favorite characters for a child's party to elegant, themed motifs for adults. The sky's the limit in terms of creativity.

Flavor Varieties: Don't feel constrained to traditional flavors. Many bakeries offer a wide range of options, from exotic fruit fillings to luxurious chocolate ganache, allowing you to tailor the cake to the birthday person's tastes.

Alternative Dessert Ideas

Cupcake Towers: A tower of cupcakes can be just as visually striking as a traditional cake and offers the added benefit of variety in flavors and decorations. Guests can choose their favorite, and you can easily cater to different dietary needs within the same display.

Dessert Bars: For a more interactive experience, consider setting up a dessert bar. Options like build-your-own sundaes, a chocolate fondue station, or a selection of miniature desserts allow guests to customize their sweet treats.

Healthy Alternatives: For health-conscious celebrants or those with dietary restrictions, alternatives like fruit arrangements, gluten-free options, or a beautifully decorated watermelon cake can be delightful and inclusive choices.

Themed Treats: Aligning desserts with your party theme can add a fun and immersive element. Think, themed cookies, macarons, or pastries that match the party's color scheme or motif.

Presentation Tips

Highlight the Dessert: Whether you opt for a traditional cake or an alternative, make sure the dessert is a focal point. Use a decorative stand, strategic lighting, or even a sprinkle of edible glitter to draw attention to the centerpiece.

Consider the Reveal: The moment the birthday dessert is presented is often a highlight. Plan for dramatic reveals with sparkler candles, themed music, or even a surprise element like a hidden design inside the cake.

Serving Considerations: Think about how your dessert choice will be served. Individual options like cupcakes or mini desserts can streamline serving, while larger cakes may require a dedicated space for cutting and plating.

Making It Memorable

Personal Touch: Incorporating a personal element, like a handmade cake topper or a special message piped on the dessert, adds a meaningful touch that celebrates the individuality of the birthday person.

Photogenic Moments: Consider how your dessert choice will photograph, ensuring those cake-cutting moments are as visually memorable as they are emotional.

Choosing the right birthday dessert, whether a traditional cake or a creative alternative, is an opportunity to express the unique tastes and personality of the honoree. By focusing on personalization, presentation, and inclusivity, you can ensure that this sweet centerpiece of the celebration is both delightful and memorable.

Managing Dietary Restrictions and Allergies

Catering to the dietary needs and allergies of your guests is a crucial aspect of party planning that ensures everyone can enjoy the celebration safely and comfortably. This consideration shows thoughtfulness and care for all attendees, making the party inclusive and enjoyable for everyone. Here's how to manage dietary restrictions and allergies effectively.

Early Identification

Gather Information: When sending out invitations, include a section where guests can note any dietary restrictions or allergies. This proactive approach allows you to plan the menu with these considerations in mind.

Clarify Needs: Dietary restrictions can range from allergies to religious or ethical dietary practices. For allergies, know the severity, as some individuals cannot tolerate cross-contamination, while others may simply prefer to avoid certain foods.

Menu Planning

Inclusive Menu: Aim to create a menu that naturally includes a variety of options catering to common dietary restrictions (gluten-free, dairy-free, vegetarian, vegan, nut-free). This approach minimizes the need for separate meals and makes everyone feel included.

Communicate with Caterers: If you're using a catering service, discuss dietary needs with them early in the planning process. Reputable caterers are accustomed to handling such requests and can often provide creative and delicious alternatives.

Labeling: For any buffet or self-serve style meal, label dishes clearly with ingredients or markers indicating if they are gluten-free, vegan, etc. This transparency allows guests to make informed choices.

Precautions for Allergies

Cross-Contamination Awareness: Be mindful of cross-contamination risks, especially with severe food allergies. Use separate utensils and serving dishes for allergen-free foods, and consider preparing these foods first to minimize exposure.

Emergency Preparedness: Have a plan in place in case of an allergic reaction, which includes knowing the location of the nearest medical facility, having contact information for all guests (or their parents, for children's parties), and keeping emergency medication like antihistamines or epinephrine injectors accessible.

Special Considerations

Homemade vs. Store-Bought: While homemade food allows for better control over ingredients, for severe allergies, sometimes store-bought products with clear ingredient labels and allergen statements are safer. Decide based on your comfort level and the specific needs of your guests.

Communication: Keep open lines of communication with guests who have dietary restrictions. Confirming the menu with them before the party can alleviate concerns and demonstrate your commitment to their safety and enjoyment.

Educate Other Guests: In cases of severe allergies (such as peanuts), inform all guests ahead of time if you're requesting they avoid bringing foods containing specific allergens to the party.

Managing dietary restrictions and allergies with diligence and care ensures a safe and inclusive environment where all guests can relax and enjoy the celebration. It reflects a level of attention and hospitality that will be appreciated by everyone attending, making the birthday party a memorable and worry-free occasion.

7

Entertainment and Activities

Entertainment Options for Different Age Groups

Selecting the right entertainment for a birthday party can transform a good celebration into an unforgettable one. However, the key to success lies in choosing activities that are age-appropriate and engaging for the guests. Here's a guide to tailoring your entertainment options to suit different age groups, ensuring everyone has a fantastic time.

For Toddlers and Preschoolers (Ages 1-4)

Interactive Storytelling: Young children love stories, especially when they come with animations, puppets, or the storyteller's engaging expressions and voices.

Bubble Shows: Few things captivate toddlers like the magic of bubbles. Bubble artists can create giant bubbles, bubble sculptures, and even place children inside bubbles, providing a mesmerizing experience.

Music and Movement: Activities that encourage dancing, jumping, and moving to music are perfect for this age group, helping them burn energy while having fun.

For Children (Ages 5-8)

Magic Shows: A magic show tailored to children, with plenty of visual tricks and audience participation, can be a highlight of the party.

Craft Stations: Set up stations where kids can make their own party favors, such as custom hats, masks, or simple jewelry. It's entertaining and gives them something to take home.

Animal Encounters: If possible, arranging for a petting zoo or a visit from someone who can safely showcase non-dangerous animals can be both educational and fun.

For Pre-Teens (Ages 9-12)

DIY Workshops: Activities like building a small robot, creating slime or a simple cooking class cater to pre-teens' desire for independence and learning new skills.

Virtual Reality Experiences: If you have access to VR headsets, set up a virtual reality gaming zone. Choose immersive experiences that are suitable for their age.

Sports and Obstacle Courses: Set up a mini sports day or an obstacle course. Activities that challenge them physically and allow for friendly competition can be a hit.

For Teenagers (Ages 13+)

Escape Rooms: Whether you hire professionals to set one up at your venue or create a DIY version, escape rooms challenge teenagers to work together to solve puzzles.

Karaoke or Lip Sync Battle: Music is a great connector for this age group. A karaoke machine or a lip-sync battle setup can provide hours of entertainment.

Movie Night: Create an outdoor cinema experience with a projector and screen or set up a cozy indoor viewing area with plenty of popcorn and snacks. Let the birthday person pick a few favorite films.

For Adults

Live Music or DJ: Music sets the atmosphere for any adult party. Whether it's a live band that can play the birthday person's favorite tunes or a DJ who knows how to keep the dance floor busy, music is a must-have.

Tasting Experiences: Wine, whiskey, or craft beer tasting sessions can be a sophisticated and enjoyable activity. Pair it with a short class on the art of tasting for an educational twist.

Interactive Games: Consider games that get everyone involved, like trivia quizzes about the birthday person or interactive game shows. These can be great ice-breakers and keep guests entertained.

When planning entertainment, always consider the space available, the overall theme of the party, and any safety requirements. By matching the entertainment to the guests' interests and developmental stages, you ensure that the party is a hit for all attendees, leaving lasting memories for the birthday person and their guests alike.

Planning and Organizing Activities and Games

Activities and games are the heart of any birthday party, injecting fun and fostering interactions among guests. A well-planned lineup can keep the energy high and ensure everyone feels included. Here's how to plan and organize activities and games that will keep your guests entertained and engaged from start to finish.

Understanding Your Audience

Age Appropriateness: Tailor the activities to the age group of the majority of your guests. What delights a child may bore a teenager, and vice versa.

Interests: If possible, choose activities that align with the interests of the birthday person and their guests. A sports-themed game might be perfect for a sports enthusiast's party, while art-related activities could be a hit at a creative individual's celebration.

Diversity in Activities

Mix It Up: Include a variety of activities that cater to different energy levels and interests. Combine high-energy games with quieter, sit-down activities to give guests options and allow for moments of rest.

Inclusivity: Ensure there are activities that everyone can participate in, regardless of physical ability or skill level. This consideration ensures no one feels left out.

Timing and Organization

Schedule Wisely: Space out activities and games throughout the party to maintain engagement and momentum. Having a rough timeline helps manage the party's pace without making it feel overly structured.

Flexibility: Be prepared to adjust the schedule based on how guests are enjoying the party. If a particular game is a hit, it might be worth extending it rather than rushing to the next scheduled activity.

Equipment and Preparation

Gather Materials: Well before the party, compile a list of all the materials and equipment you'll need for each game or activity. Ensure everything is prepared and ready to go to avoid last-minute scrambles.

Safety First: For any activity, especially those that are physical, consider the safety of participants. Have first aid supplies on hand, and ensure the play area is free from hazards.

Facilitation and Participation

Clear Instructions: When introducing a game or activity, explain the rules clearly and concisely. It might help to demonstrate or have a trial run to ensure everyone understands.

Encourage Participation: Foster an atmosphere where everyone feels comfortable joining in. This might mean participating yourself to get things started or gently encouraging shyer guests.

Memorable Highlights

Signature Activity: Consider having one standout activity that ties into the party's theme, serving as a memorable highlight. This could be a custom escape room, a DIY craft that aligns with the theme, or a unique game tailored to the birthday person's interests.

Prizes and Rewards: Offering small prizes can add a competitive edge to games, but ensure that the focus remains on fun rather than winning. Prizes can also be given for participation to encourage everyone to join in.

Documentation

Capture the Fun: Assign someone the role of photographer or videographer to capture moments of joy and engagement during the activities. These images and videos become precious keepsakes, reminding everyone of the fun long after the party ends.

Planning and organizing activities and games for a birthday party requires thoughtfulness and flexibility. By considering your audience, preparing thoroughly, and fostering an inclusive and engaging environment, you can ensure that the entertainment is a highlight of the celebration, cherished by the birthday person and their guests alike.

Hiring Professionals: DJs, Magicians, Entertainers

Incorporating professional entertainers such as DJs, magicians, or other performers can elevate a birthday party, making it an unforgettable experience for the guest of honor and attendees. These professionals bring expertise, excitement, and engagement, ensuring the entertainment smoothly integrates with the theme and flow of the event. Here's a guide to selecting and working with professional entertainers.

Identifying the Right Entertainment

Match the Party Theme and Audience: The type of professional entertainer you choose should complement the party's theme and be appropriate for the age group of your guests. A magician might be perfect for a children's party, while a DJ could be better suited for a teenager or adult celebration.

Research and Recommendations: Look for entertainers with excellent reviews or those recommended by people you trust. Professional websites, social media platforms, and entertainment agencies can be valuable resources for finding and vetting potential entertainers.

Booking Process

Early Engagement: High-quality entertainers often book up quickly, especially during peak seasons. Reach out well in advance of your party date to secure your preferred professional.

Clear Communication: Discuss your expectations, the theme, the age group of the guests, and any specific requests you have with the entertainer. Ensure they are comfortable and experienced in handling such requirements.

Confirm Details: Before finalizing the booking, confirm the duration of the performance, setup needs, the space required, and any technical specifications. Also, discuss their policy on guest interaction and participation.

Contract and Expectations

Formal Agreement: A contract should outline the performance details, including the date, time, duration, fees, cancellation policy, and any special requests. This document protects both parties and clarifies expectations.

Deposit and Payment Terms: Understand the payment structure, including deposit requirements and final payment due dates. Clarify any additional costs, such as travel expenses or special equipment.

Preparing for the Performance

Venue Coordination: If your party is at an external venue, coordinate with the venue management to ensure the entertainer's needs can be accommodated, such as electrical outlets for a DJ or a stage area for a magician.

Day-of Contact: Provide the entertainer with a day-of contact person and phone number for any last-minute coordination or issues that may arise.

Setup Time: Allow ample time for the entertainer to set up and sound check before guests arrive, ensuring the performance goes smoothly.

During the Event

Introductions: Briefly introduce the entertainer to your guests to establish a connection and build anticipation for the performance.

Audience Engagement: Professional entertainers are skilled at reading the room and engaging with the audience. Trust their expertise, but also be available to assist if there are any unforeseen issues or needs.

Post-Performance

Feedback: After the event, providing feedback to the entertainer can be beneficial for both parties. Positive comments can be used as testimonials, while constructive feedback helps professionals refine their performances.

Gratitude: A simple thank you, whether in person or via follow-up communication, acknowledges the entertainer's role in making your party a success.

Hiring professional entertainers like DJs, magicians, or other performers can significantly enhance the enjoyment and atmosphere of a birthday party. By carefully selecting, booking, and working with these professionals, you ensure not just seamless entertainment but also create lasting memories for everyone involved.

8

Party Favors and Gifts

Ideas for Memorable Party Favors

Party favors are a lovely way to thank your guests for joining the celebration and to leave them with a tangible memory of the special day. Choosing favors that resonate with the party theme, the interests of the birthday person, or the collective tastes of the guests can turn these small gifts into cherished keepsakes. Here are some creative and memorable party favor ideas for guests of all ages.

For Children's Parties

Customized Activity Books: Create activity books tailored to the party theme. Include coloring pages, puzzles, and games. This not only keeps the theme going but also gives children a fun activity to take home.

DIY Craft Kits: Assemble small kits with materials for a simple craft or project. This can be particularly engaging, as it allows children to extend the party fun to their own time and space.

Themed Goodie Bags: Fill bags with small toys, stickers, and treats that match the party theme. Personalize each bag with the guest's name to add a special touch.

For Pre-Teens and Teenagers

Tech Accessories: Small, tech-related items like earbud headphones, funky USB drives, or phone stands are both practical and trendy, making them perfect for this age group.

Eco-Friendly Gadgets: Consider giving out reusable water bottles, bamboo toothbrushes, or plantable seed paper. These eco-conscious gifts can be both thoughtful and useful.

DIY Beauty Kits: Small kits with ingredients for making their own lip balm, bath bombs, or face masks can offer a fun, at-home activity.

For Adults

Gourmet Goodies: Small jars of homemade preserves, gourmet salts, or a mix for a special cocktail can cater to adult tastes. Pair these with a recipe card for a personal touch.

Plant Starters: Small succulents or herbs in personalized pots offer a lasting reminder of the celebration. They're both decorative and practical, appealing to guests' green thumbs.

Personalized Keepsakes: Items like engraved keychains, custom coasters, or monogrammed candles can serve as elegant mementos of the occasion.

Universal Ideas

Photo Memories: Set up a photo booth with props related to the party theme.

Give guests their photo prints in a personalized frame or with a thank-you note as a memento.

Customized Merchandise: T-shirts, hats, or tote bags featuring a design or slogan from the party can be both unique and useful. For a more budget-friendly option, consider buttons or magnets.

Sweet Treats: Artisanal chocolates, a mini cake-in-a-jar, or beautifully decorated cookies can delight guests of any age. Customize the packaging with the party theme and date.

Presentation Tips

Packaging Matters: Invest time in how the favors are presented. Creative packaging that aligns with the party theme can make even simple favors feel special.

Personalization: Adding a personal touch, like a handwritten thank-you note or a custom label, shows appreciation and thoughtfulness.

Display Creatively: Integrate the party favors into the event decor. Setting up a favor station where guests can choose their items or packaging them as part of the table settings can add to the party's aesthetic.

Choosing the right party favors requires considering the interests of your guests and finding a balance between creativity, budget, and practicality. With thoughtful selection and presentation, these small tokens of appreciation can leave a lasting impression, making your party memorable long after it ends.

Organizing a Gift Table or Wishlist

A well-organized gift table or a thoughtfully curated wishlist can streamline the gift-giving process for a birthday celebration, making it easier for guests to select meaningful presents and for the host to manage them during the event. Here's how to approach organizing a gift table and creating a wishlist that respects the preferences of the birthday person while ensuring a smooth experience for the guests.

Organizing a Gift Table

Strategic Placement: Set up the gift table near the entrance where it's easily accessible yet out of the way of high-traffic areas. Ensure it's clearly visible and marked with a tastefully designed sign.

Decor and Theme Alignment: Decorate the gift table to match the party's theme. This doesn't have to be elaborate—a few thematic touches can integrate the table into the overall decor seamlessly.

Instructions for Guests: If there are specific instructions for the gifts (e.g., unwrapped for a display shower or labeled for a later opening), clearly communicate this both prior to the event and at the table itself.

Gift Tracking: Provide a notebook or digital system next to the gift table for guests to write down their names and the gifts they brought. This makes sending personalized thank-you notes afterward much easier.

Creating and Sharing a Wishlist

Use Online Platforms: Online wishlists are convenient and can be easily shared with guests through email or event social media pages. Platforms like Amazon, MyRegistry.com, or dedicated event planning sites allow for a wide range of items from different stores.

Diversify Options: Include items across a broad range of price points to accommodate different budgets. Consider adding experiences or charitable donations as part of the wishlist for guests who prefer giving non-material gifts.

Communicate Tactfully: When sharing the wishlist, emphasize that gifts are appreciated but not obligatory. The primary goal is to celebrate together, and their presence at the party is gift enough.

Update Regularly: If possible, keep the wishlist updated to reflect items that have already been purchased, which helps prevent duplicate gifts and ensures guests know what's still available to choose from.

Etiquette Tips

Gift Opening Protocol: Decide whether gifts will be opened during the party and plan accordingly. If so, schedule a specific time for this, ensuring it doesn't overshadow other activities. For adult parties or in cases where time doesn't allow, consider opening gifts privately and sending thank-you notes later.

Thank-You Notes: Regardless of the size or nature of the gift, sending a thank-you note is a must. Personalize each note to reflect the gift received and the thoughtfulness of the gesture.

Handling Group Gifts: If friends or family members are going in on a group gift, provide a way for them to coordinate this, either through a designated person or an online platform where they can contribute.

Organizing a gift table and managing a wishlist requires attention to detail and consideration for both the birthday person's preferences and the guests' convenience. By following these guidelines, you can ensure that the gift-giving aspect of the party enhances the celebration and shows appreciation for the thoughtfulness of the guests.

Etiquette for Gift Opening

The moment of opening gifts at a birthday party can be filled with excitement and gratitude, but navigating it requires a bit of etiquette to ensure it remains a positive experience for both the birthday person and their guests. Here's how to approach gift opening with grace and tact.

Timing and Setting

Choose an Appropriate Time: If you decide to open gifts during the party, choose a time when all or most guests have arrived and are settled in but before the party starts winding down. This ensures everyone who brings a gift can see the joy their gift brings.

Create a Comfortable Setting: Arrange seating in a way that all guests can see the gift opening without crowding. The birthday person should have a designated spot, perhaps elevated or central, to open gifts.

The Art of Gracious Gift Opening

Expressing Gratitude: Teach the birthday person, especially if they're a child, the importance of saying thank you for each gift, regardless of what it is. It's the thought and effort that count.

Tactful Reactions: Encourage genuine reactions but also tactfulness. If the gift is a duplicate or not exactly to their taste, focusing on the thoughtfulness of the gesture is key. Phrases like "Thank you, I really appreciate it!" can never go wrong.

Involving Guests: Make the gift-opening interactive by allowing guests to hand their gifts to the birthday person personally if they wish. This adds a personal touch and lets the giver explain their gift if they desire.

Managing the Process

Gift Tracker: Assign someone the task of tracking who gave each gift. This makes sending personalized thank-you notes easier and ensures no one is accidentally overlooked.

Pace Yourself: Especially for parties with many guests, gift opening can become lengthy. Keep the pace brisk but not rushed, allowing for a brief appreciation of each gift.

Special Considerations

Sensitive Situations: If there's a significant discrepancy in the value or thoughtfulness of gifts, it's important to handle the situation delicately. Emphasize the appreciation for everyone's presence and contributions to the celebration, not just the material gifts.

Post-Event Acknowledgement: In cases where gifts are not opened during the event, consider sending photos of the birthday person with the gifts to the respective givers along with the thank-you notes. This can make the giver feel appreciated and included in the moment.

Thank-You Notes

Promptness: Aim to send out thank-you notes promptly after the party. Within a week is ideal, but up to two weeks is generally acceptable for larger events.

Personalization: Personalize each note to reflect the specific gift and the relationship to the giver. This personal touch shows genuine appreciation and strengthens relationships.

The gift-opening segment of a birthday party, handled with care and etiquette, can amplify the joy and communal spirit of the celebration. By focusing on gratitude, inclusivity, and tact, both the birthday person and their guests can enjoy this tradition as a highlight of the event.

9

Capturing the Memories

Hiring a Photographer or Setting Up a DIY Photo Booth

Capturing the joy and special moments of a birthday party is essential, leaving you and your guests with tangible memories to cherish. Deciding between hiring a professional photographer or setting up a DIY photo booth—or perhaps opting for both—depends on the nature of the event and what you hope to achieve. Here's a guide to making the best choice for your celebration.

Hiring a Professional Photographer

Pros:

Quality and Expertise: A professional brings experience and skill, ensuring high-quality images that capture the essence and emotion of the party. They know how to work with lighting, composition, and timing to get the best shots.

Comprehensive Coverage: Photographers can document the entire event, from candid moments to group shots, without missing out on key events like the blowing of the candles or the opening of gifts.

Stress-Free Experience: Hiring a professional means you can enjoy the party without worrying about capturing moments. You're free to be fully present, knowing that the photography is in capable hands.

Cons:

Cost: Professional photography services can be a significant addition to your party budget.

Less Spontaneity: While professionals capture the event beautifully, the presence of a photographer might inhibit some guests, potentially affecting the spontaneity of the images.

Setting Up a DIY Photo Booth

Pros:

Fun and Engaging: A photo booth with props and backdrops aligned with the party theme can be a fun activity, encouraging guests to get creative and have fun.

Customization: You can tailor the booth to match the party theme perfectly, from the backdrop to the props and even the photo frames.

Affordability: A DIY photo booth can be put together at a relatively low cost, especially if you're creative with materials and use a digital camera or smartphone.

Cons:

Requires Management: You'll need to set up and manage the booth, which might include troubleshooting any technical issues or encouraging guests to use it.

Variable Quality: The quality of the photos will depend on the equipment used and the lighting conditions. Unlike professional photos, DIY booth images may be more about the fun than high-quality results.

Tips for Both Options

Combine for Best Results: Budget permitting, combining a professional photographer with a DIY photo booth can offer the best of both worlds: professional-quality images and a fun, engaging activity for guests.

Photo Booth as a Guest Book: Encourage guests to leave a copy of their photo booth picture along with a message as a modern take on a guest book. This can be a wonderful keepsake for the birthday person.

Sharing Photos Post-Event: Whether taken by a professional or snapped in your photo booth, make sure to share the photos with your guests after the event. Online albums, social media, or personalized thank-you notes with photos are great ways to relive and share the joy.

Choosing between a professional photographer and a DIY photo booth—or incorporating both—will depend on your priorities, budget, and the overall vibe you want for your party. Each option offers unique benefits, from capturing high-quality memories to adding an interactive element that guests can enjoy.

Encouraging Guest Participation in Capturing Moments

In the digital age, everyone has the potential to be a photographer with their smartphone. Encouraging guests to capture and share their own moments from the birthday celebration can complement professional photos or a DIY photo booth, offering a variety of perspectives and candid memories of the event. Here's how to encourage and organize guest participation in capturing and sharing these precious moments.

Creating a Shared Album or Hashtag

Social Media Hashtag: Create a unique hashtag for the birthday party and encourage guests to use it when posting photos on social media. This allows everyone to view and share the celebration's moments from different angles.

Digital Album Platforms: Utilize platforms like Google Photos or Dropbox to create a shared album where guests can upload their pictures and videos. Ensure you provide clear instructions on how to access and contribute to the album.

Encouraging Participation

Announcement at the Party: Make a brief announcement reminding guests to capture moments they enjoy and how to share those with everyone via the hashtag or digital album.

Signage: Place signs around the party venue with the hashtag and instructions for the digital album. This can serve as a constant reminder and encourage guests to snap and share photos throughout the event.

Engagement: Encourage guests to capture not just posed group shots but also candid moments, decorations, and other unique aspects of the party. These often make for the most memorable and genuine photos.

Making It Fun and Interactive

Photo Challenges: Create a photo challenge or scavenger hunt with specific moments or items to capture, adding a fun and interactive element to the photography.

Props and Photo Spots: Set up specific spots around the venue that are perfect for photos, such as a themed backdrop or an interesting piece of decor. Provide fun props to encourage creative and playful shots.

Post-Event Sharing

Thank You Notes: When sending out thank you notes post-party, include a reminder of the shared album or where to find the photos on social media. You could also highlight some favorite shots in the note.

Slideshow: After the event, compile a selection of guest-captured photos into a slideshow to share with the attendees. This can be a lovely way to relive the party and appreciate the different perspectives.

Privacy Considerations

Respect Privacy: Make it clear that guests should only share photos they have permission to post, especially when children are involved. Respect guests' wishes if they prefer not to have their photos shared publicly.

Sensitive Content: Remind guests to be mindful of the content they capture and share, ensuring it's appropriate and in keeping with the spirit of the celebration.

By actively encouraging guest participation in capturing moments, you enrich the collection of memories from the birthday party. This inclusive approach not only diversifies the perspectives and scenes captured but also fosters a sense of community and shared experience among your guests, making the event even more memorable.

Ideas for Sharing Photos and Videos Post-Party

After a memorable birthday celebration, sharing the photos and videos with guests is a wonderful way to relive the fun and keep the joyful memories alive. Here are creative and thoughtful ways to share these precious moments, ensuring everyone can enjoy the highlights of the party long after the last balloon has popped.

Digital Albums and Galleries

Online Photo Galleries: Utilize platforms like Google Photos, Flickr, or Dropbox to create shared albums. These platforms often allow for easy uploading, organizing, and sharing with a link, making it accessible for all guests to view and download their favorite moments.

Personalized Website: For a special touch, create a website dedicated to the birthday celebration. Include photo galleries, video clips, and maybe a blog post recounting the event highlights. This can serve as a digital keepsake for the birthday person.

Social Media Shares

Hashtag Recap: If you used a unique hashtag for the event, compile a post-party recap featuring a selection of photos and videos tagged by guests. This can be shared on your social media profiles or a dedicated event page.

Facebook Album: Create a comprehensive album on Facebook and tag attendees, encouraging them to tag themselves and comment on their favorite moments. This can foster a sense of community and shared joy among the guests.

Video Montages and Slideshows

Highlight Reel: Compile the best moments into a short video montage or slideshow. Tools like iMovie, Canva, or Adobe Spark make it easy to add music, transitions, and captions to create something truly special.

Personalized Messages: Consider adding personalized thank you messages or shoutouts within the video to make it even more memorable for guests.

Personalized Thank You Notes

Photo Thank You Cards: Select a few standout photos from the party and use them to create personalized thank you cards. This tangible memento is a heartfelt way to express your gratitude for their presence and contribution to the celebration.

Emails with Links: For a more digital approach, send out thank you emails with links to the photo album or video montage. You can use this opportunity to express your thanks and share a personal message about the shared memories.

Interactive Shares

QR Codes: Print QR codes on thank you cards or post-party communications that direct guests to the online album or highlight reel. It's a modern and engaging way to share memories.

Collaborative Playlists: If music was a big part of the celebration, share a collaborative playlist with songs from the party. Include a link to the photo album or video montage in the playlist description for a multimedia experience.

Printed Photo Books

Custom Photo Books: For milestone birthdays, consider creating a custom photo book with highlights from the celebration. This can be a beautiful keepsake for the birthday person and a unique gift for close family members or friends.

Special Considerations

Privacy and Permissions: Always ensure you have permission to share photos and videos, especially when children are involved. Respect guests' privacy preferences and consider using platforms that allow for password protection or restricted access.

Sharing photos and videos post-party is not just about distributing images; it's about continuing the celebration, deepening connections among guests, and creating lasting tokens of appreciation. By choosing a thoughtful and creative approach to sharing these memories, you ensure that the joy of the celebration lives on.

10

Day-of Party Checklist

Final Preparations and Setup

The final stretch before the birthday party involves a flurry of activity, from ensuring the venue is ready, to confirming that all elements align with your vision. Effective final preparations and setup are crucial for a smooth celebration, allowing you to enjoy the event with minimal stress. Here's a comprehensive checklist to guide you through these last crucial steps.

Venue Preparation

Venue Walk through: Conduct a final walk through of the venue a day or two before the party to visualize the space and confirm that all arrangements meet your expectations.

Decoration Setup: Plan to decorate the venue several hours before the party starts. This includes setting up tables, arranging seating, and placing decorations. If using balloons, remember they should be inflated on the day of the party to look their best.

Signage and Directions: Place signs or balloons at key points to guide guests to the venue or specific areas like the gift table, bathrooms, and activity stations.

Entertainment and Activities

Confirm with Entertainers: Reconfirm arrival times and any special requirements with DJs, magicians, or other entertainers. Ensure there's a clear setup area for them and that any necessary electrical outlets are accessible.

Activity Stations: Set up any DIY activity stations or game areas, making sure all materials are ready and instructions (if needed) are clear and visible.

Food and Beverage

Catering Confirmation: If using a catering service, confirm the menu, headcount, and delivery or setup time. Make sure there's a designated area for food setup and that it's equipped with the necessary tables, utensils, and serving dishes.

DIY Food Preparations: For homemade food, finalize preparations and ensure cold items are stored properly. Label dishes with ingredients if accommodating dietary restrictions.

Final Details

Emergency Kit: Prepare a small emergency kit with items like tape, scissors, a first-aid kit, extra batteries, and any other last-minute fix-it tools.

Guest Comfort: Check the venue for comfort. Adjust heating or cooling as needed and ensure there are enough seating areas for guests.

Safety Measures: Review safety measures, especially if there are candles involved in your decor or if the party includes small items that could be hazardous to younger guests.

Day-Of Timeline

Create a Timeline: Draft a timeline for the day of the party, including setup, guest arrival, meal times, entertainment slots, and any special moments like cake cutting or speeches. Share this with any helpers, vendors, or entertainers to ensure everyone is on the same page.

Assign Roles: If friends or family are helping, assign specific roles to them, such as managing the music, overseeing the food area, or greeting guests. This helps distribute tasks and lets you focus on hosting.

Last-Minute Checks

Functionality Check: Test equipment like sound systems, lighting, or photo booths to ensure everything is working correctly.

Cleanliness Check: Ensure the venue is clean, with tidy bathrooms and a well-arranged dining or party area.

Relaxation Moment: Once everything is set up, take a few moments to relax and compose yourself before the guests arrive. Remember to enjoy the celebration you've worked hard to organize.

Efficient final preparations and setup are the keys to a seamless birthday celebration. By methodically checking off these tasks, you ensure that the party environment is welcoming, fun, and ready for an unforgettable celebration.

Coordinating Vendors and Helpers

Smooth collaboration with vendors and helpers is crucial for the seamless execution of a birthday party. Effective coordination ensures that every component—from catering to entertainment—comes together perfectly, allowing you to focus on celebrating with your guests. Here's how to manage these collaborations effectively

Establishing Clear Communication

Pre-Event Meetings: Schedule final meetings or calls with all vendors and key helpers a week before the event. Confirm details such as arrival times, setup needs, and specific responsibilities.

Contact List: Compile a list of contact information for all vendors and helpers. Distribute this list among your team and key family members or friends involved in the party planning.

Detailed Briefings for Vendors and Helpers

Expectations and Timelines: Provide a detailed schedule of the event, highlighting when and where each vendor is expected to deliver, set up, and break down. Include any specific instructions related to the venue or event flow.

Roles and Responsibilities: Clearly define the roles for each helper. Whether it's overseeing the guest sign-in table, managing the music playlist, or coordinating games and activities, ensure everyone knows their tasks.

Coordination Tools and Techniques

Event Management Apps: Utilize event management apps or tools to keep track of tasks, schedules, and communications. These tools can be invaluable for real-time updates and checklists.

Walkie-Talkies or Group Chats: For larger venues or teams, consider using walkie-talkies, creating a group chat, or using apps for quick and easy communication during the event.

On-Site Management

Early Arrival: Encourage vendors and helpers to arrive early for setup. This gives you a buffer for addressing any unexpected issues that may arise.

Check-In System: Set up a check-in process for vendors and helpers on the day of the party to ensure everyone arrives as planned and knows where to go.

Designated Coordinator: If possible, designate a trusted friend, family member, or professional event coordinator as the point person for questions or issues. This allows you to enjoy the party without being pulled away for logistical concerns.

Problem-Solving and Flexibility

Contingency Plans: Have backup plans for critical elements like food, music, and entertainment. Knowing your options in case of a vendor cancellation or technical issue can alleviate stress.

Empower Decision-Making: Allow your helpers and vendors some level of autonomy to make small decisions on the spot. Trusting their expertise can lead to smoother operations.

Post-Event Debrief

Feedback Session: After the party, consider having a debrief session with key helpers and vendors. Discuss what went well and areas for improvement. This feedback can be invaluable for planning future events.

Gratitude: Express your appreciation for their hard work and contribution to the event's success. Thank-you notes, online reviews, or small gifts are thoughtful ways to show your gratitude.

Coordinating vendors and helpers effectively is about clear communication, detailed planning, and building a team atmosphere. By taking these steps, you can ensure that each aspect of the party is handled professionally and smoothly, leading to a successful and stress-free celebration.

Ensuring a Smooth Flow of Events

A well-organized birthday party not only creates a memorable experience for the guest of honor and attendees but also showcases the thoughtful planning behind it. Ensuring a smooth flow of events is key to maintaining energy and engagement throughout the celebration. Here's how to orchestrate the festivities for seamless execution.

Creating a Detailed Schedule

Timeline: Develop a detailed timeline that includes the start and end times of the party, along with the timing for specific activities, meals, entertainment, and any special moments like speeches or cake cutting. This timeline acts as a guide for both planning and execution.

Flexibility: While it's important to have a schedule, remain flexible. Allow for spontaneous moments and adjust as needed based on the party's dynamics and guest engagement.

Coordinating with Vendors and Helpers

Pre-Event Briefing: Hold a briefing session with all vendors and helpers to walk through the timeline and their specific roles. This ensures everyone knows their responsibilities and how they fit into the overall flow of the party.

Point Person: Designate a reliable point person to oversee the schedule and troubleshoot any issues that arise. This person should be well-informed about all aspects of the party and empowered to make decisions.

Managing Transitions

Cue Systems: Establish clear cues for transitions between different parts of the event. This could involve audio cues, verbal announcements, or signals to vendors and helpers to initiate the next activity.

Engage Guests: During transitions, have a plan to keep guests engaged. This could be background music, a slideshow of photos, or a simple interactive activity that doesn't require full attention.

Guest Considerations

Announcements: Make periodic announcements to guide guests through the party. Whether it's moving to the dining area, gathering for a group photo, or inviting guests to participate in an activity, clear communication helps manage guest flow.

Signage: Use signs to indicate different areas (e.g., restrooms, activity stations, food and drinks). This helps guests navigate the space independently and reduces confusion.

Handling Delays and Unforeseen Issues

Backup Plans: Have backup plans for critical elements of the party. If an entertainer is late, for example, be prepared to fill the gap with another activity or extend a current one.

Stay Calm and Positive: Your demeanor sets the tone for the event. Handling any hiccups with calmness and a positive attitude reassures guests and keeps the atmosphere enjoyable.

Wrapping Up

Closing Announcement: As the party nears its end, make a closing announcement thanking guests for their attendance and noting any final activities or reminders (e.g., taking party favors, final photo opportunities).

Feedback Loop: After the event, reflect on what went well and what could be improved. This feedback is invaluable for planning future events.

Ensuring a smooth flow of events requires meticulous planning, effective communication, and the ability to adapt to the unexpected. By implementing these strategies, you can create a well-organized and enjoyable birthday celebration that flows effortlessly from start to finish.

11

Safety and Comfort

Ensuring Safety and Comfort

Ensuring the safety and comfort of all guests is paramount when hosting a birthday party. From preparing the venue to anticipate potential hazards, to making sure every attendee feels welcomed and at ease, these considerations are vital for a successful and enjoyable event. Here's how to prioritize safety and comfort throughout your celebration.

Venue Safety Checks

Conduct a Pre-Event Inspection: Walk through the venue to identify and mitigate potential hazards. Look for trip hazards, ensure all areas are well-lit, and check that emergency exits are clearly marked and unobstructed.

Weather Preparedness: For outdoor events, have contingency plans for adverse weather conditions. This might include having tents, heaters, or fans available, and a backup indoor location if necessary.

Food Safety

Dietary Accommodations: Clearly label food items, especially those containing common allergens, and provide alternatives for guests with dietary restrictions to ensure everyone can enjoy the meal safely.

Proper Food Handling: If handling food yourself, follow food safety guidelines to prevent foodborne illnesses. This includes keeping hot foods hot and cold foods cold, using separate utensils for different dishes, and avoiding cross-contamination.

Child Safety

Childproofing: If children are attending, childproof the venue by securing gates, covering electrical outlets, and placing breakable or hazardous items out of reach.

Supervised Activities: Ensure all activities are supervised by responsible adults, especially those that might involve risks, such as swimming pools or trampolines.

Comfort Considerations

Seating Arrangements: Provide ample and comfortable seating for guests. Consider the needs of elderly guests or those with mobility issues, ensuring they have easy access to seating, restrooms, and shaded or indoor areas.

Temperature Control: Keep the venue at a comfortable temperature. For indoor venues, adjust the heating or air conditioning as needed. For outdoor events, provide options for guests to cool down or warm up.

Accessibility

Ensure Accessibility: Make sure the venue is accessible to everyone, including guests with wheelchairs or strollers. This includes accessible parking, entrance ramps, and restrooms.

Inclusive Planning: When planning activities and entertainment, include options that are accessible to guests of all abilities.

Emergency Preparedness

First Aid Kit: Have a well-stocked first aid kit on hand, and familiarize yourself with basic first aid procedures. Inform helpers or co-hosts where the kit is located.

Point of Contact: Designate a point of contact for emergencies. This person should be aware of the nearest hospital, have a list of emergency contacts for guests (particularly for children), and know how to reach local emergency services.

Open Communication

Provide Clear Information: Before the event, provide guests with information about parking, the venue's layout, and any specific safety instructions. Include details on how to communicate needs or concerns during the party.

Feedback Loop: Encourage guests to share any comfort or safety concerns with you or a designated helper during the event, ensuring everyone feels heard and cared for.

By proactively addressing safety and comfort, you create an environment where guests can relax and enjoy the celebration to its fullest. These efforts show your guests that their well-being is a top priority, contributing to a positive and memorable party experience.

Planning for Different Weather Conditions

Weather can be unpredictable, and when planning a birthday party, especially one that involves outdoor elements, it's crucial to have plans in place for various weather scenarios. Being prepared for different weather conditions ensures that the celebration goes smoothly, regardless of what Mother Nature has in store. Here's how to make your party weatherproof.

Monitoring Weather Forecasts

Stay Informed: Start checking the weather forecast a week in advance and more frequently as the party date approaches. Use reliable sources and consider consulting local weather stations for the most accurate predictions.

Preparing for Sunshine and Heat

Shade Solutions: Ensure there are shaded areas available for guests to cool off. Renting tents, setting up umbrellas, or utilizing natural shade can provide relief from the sun.

Hydration Stations: Set up stations with water and refreshing beverages to keep guests hydrated. Consider adding fans or misters in particularly hot areas to cool down the environment.

Sun Protection: Offer sunscreen and have a few spare hats or visors available for guests who may have forgotten theirs.

Handling Rain or Wind

Indoor Backup Plan: Always have an accessible indoor space ready in case of rain. This could be a rented venue, a home, or a sheltered pavilion in a park.

Weatherproof Decor: If there's a chance of wind or rain, ensure your decorations are secured and won't be damaged by wet conditions. Use weights for balloons and sturdy, waterproof materials where possible.

Communication Plan: Have a plan for informing guests of any last-minute location changes due to weather, whether through text, email, or a designated social media page.

Coping with Cold Weather

Warmth Areas: For chilly days, rent outdoor heaters, provide blankets, or set up a fire pit (safety permitting) where guests can gather to stay warm.

Hot Beverages: Offer a selection of hot beverages like coffee, tea, or hot chocolate to keep guests cozy.

Enclosed Spaces: If using tents, consider sides to enclose the area and retain heat. Ensure any heating devices are safely positioned and operated.

All-Weather Preparedness

Emergency Kit: Have a weather emergency kit on hand, including ponchos, extra umbrellas, towels, and a first aid kit.

Flooring Solutions: For outdoor parties, consider the terrain. Use outdoor rugs, mats, or temporary flooring to prevent slipping in wet conditions and to protect against uneven or muddy ground.

Insurance: For large or particularly significant events, look into event insurance that covers weather-related cancellations. This can provide peace of mind and financial protection.

By planning for different weather conditions, you demonstrate foresight and care for your guests' comfort and safety. These strategies not only minimize weather-related disruptions but also ensure that your birthday celebration remains enjoyable, come rain or shine.

Accessibility and Accommodation for All Guests

Creating an inclusive and welcoming environment for all guests, regardless of their physical abilities or needs, is a key aspect of thoughtful party planning. Ensuring accessibility and providing accommodations not only reflects consideration and respect for every attendee but also enhances the overall enjoyment of the event. Here's how to plan your birthday party with accessibility and accommodation in mind.

Venue Accessibility

Choose an Accessible Venue: Select a venue that is accessible to guests with mobility challenges, including those who use wheelchairs, walkers, or strollers. Features to look for include ramp access, wide doorways, accessible restrooms, and ample parking close to the entrance.

Seating Arrangements: Ensure there is comfortable seating available and that the layout accommodates easy movement for guests with mobility aids. Consider reserving seats for guests who may need to sit closer to restrooms or exits.

Sensory Considerations

Quiet Zones: For guests who may be overwhelmed by noise or crowds, designate a quiet area where they can retreat and relax. This space should be away from the main party activities and comfortably furnished.

Adjusting Sensory Inputs: Be mindful of lighting and sound levels, especially if you know your guests include individuals with sensory sensitivities. Avoid strobe lights and overly loud music, or offer headphones for noise reduction.

Dietary Accommodations

Communicate with Guests: When sending invitations, ask guests to inform you of any dietary restrictions or allergies. This ensures everyone can safely enjoy the food and drinks offered.

Label Food and Drink Options: Clearly label food items with ingredients or symbols indicating if they are gluten-free, nut-free, dairy-free, vegetarian, or vegan. Consider offering a separate menu or options for guests with specific dietary needs.

Providing Information and Assistance

Event Information: Provide detailed information about the event ahead of time, including accessibility features, what to expect during the party, and who to contact for assistance. This can help guests with disabilities or special needs to prepare and feel comfortable attending.

On-Site Assistance: Have a designated person or team available to assist guests who may need help navigating the venue, accessing facilities, or participating in activities. Make sure these helpers are easily identifiable.

Inclusive Activities and Entertainment

Choose Inclusive Activities: Plan activities that can be enjoyed by guests of all abilities. Offer alternative ways to participate for those who may not be able to engage in certain games or physical activities.

Personalized Accommodations: For activities that require movement or specific skills, have adaptations ready, such as modified rules or equipment, to ensure everyone can join in the fun.

Continuous Improvement

Feedback and Learning: After the event, seek feedback from guests about the accessibility and accommodations provided. This can offer valuable insights for making future events even more inclusive and enjoyable for everyone.

Planning with accessibility and accommodation in mind is about more than just meeting basic needs; it's about creating a genuinely inclusive atmosphere where all guests feel valued and able to fully participate in the celebration. By taking these steps, you ensure that your birthday party is a welcoming and enjoyable experience for every guest.

12

The After-Party

Cleaning Up: Strategies and Tips

The culmination of a successful birthday party often leaves behind a less glamorous aftermath — the cleanup. Efficiently tackling this task ensures the venue is returned to its original state and helps minimize stress post-celebration. Here are strategies and tips for a smooth and effective cleanup process.

Plan Ahead for Cleanup

Designate a Cleanup Crew: Assemble a team of helpers in advance. Friends, family members, or hired staff can share the workload, making cleanup quicker and more manageable.

Prepare Cleaning Supplies: Gather all necessary cleaning supplies beforehand. This includes trash bags, recycling bins, cleaning sprays, paper towels, gloves, and any other items specific to the venue's requirements.

During the Party

Stay Organized: Maintain a level of tidiness throughout the event. Use clearly labeled bins for trash, recycling, and food waste to encourage guests to dispose of items properly.

Immediate Spill Management: Address spills and accidents as they happen to prevent stains and reduce hazards.

Post-Party Cleanup Strategies

Break Down the Tasks: Divide the cleanup tasks among the crew, focusing on different areas or types of tasks (e.g., collecting decorations, managing waste, cleaning surfaces).

Start with Trash and Recycling: Clearing away trash, recycling, and food waste first can dramatically reduce the overall mess and make further cleaning tasks easier.

Decorations and Rentals: Carefully take down decorations to save or repurpose for future events. Check rental agreements for specific return conditions and organize items accordingly.

Efficient Cleaning Methods

Top-to-Bottom Approach: When cleaning surfaces, start from the top (e.g., countertops, tables) and work your way down to the floor, so you're not redoing work.

Focus on High-Traffic Areas: Prioritize cleaning areas that were most used during the party, such as dining areas, bathrooms, and activity stations.

Floor Care: Sweep or vacuum all floors. Mop if necessary, especially in areas prone to spills or heavy foot traffic.

Reducing Waste and Environmental Impact

Repurpose and Recycle: Separate materials that can be recycled or repurposed. Consider donating leftover food to local shelters if safe and permissible.

Sustainable Cleaning Products: Use eco-friendly cleaning products to minimize environmental impact. Natural alternatives like vinegar and baking soda can be effective for many cleaning tasks.

After Cleanup

Venue Walkthrough: Conduct a final walkthrough of the venue to ensure nothing is missed and that the space is left in good condition.

Return Keys and Security Checks: If you rented a venue, make sure to return keys or access cards. Check that all doors and windows are secure, and lights and electronic equipment are turned off.

Show Appreciation

Thank Your Cleanup Crew: Acknowledge the efforts of everyone who helped with the cleanup. A simple thank you, a group meal, or small tokens of appreciation can go a long way.

Cleaning up after a birthday party doesn't have to be a daunting task. With preparation, teamwork, and efficient strategies, you can tackle the cleanup process smoothly and effectively, wrapping up the celebration on a positive note.

Sending Thank You Notes

Sending thank you notes after a birthday party is more than a polite gesture—it's a heartfelt way to express gratitude to guests for their presence, gifts, and contributions to making the celebration special. In our fast-paced, digital world, a thoughtful thank you note can leave a lasting impression. Here's how to craft and send thank you notes that resonate with your guests.

Start with a List

Compile a Guest List: Ensure you have a complete list of attendees, including those who may have sent gifts but couldn't attend. This list will be your guide to ensuring no one is forgotten.

Personalize Each Note

Personal Touch: Personalize each note by mentioning the specific gift or how the guest contributed to the party (e.g., helping with decorations, bringing food). This personal acknowledgment shows genuine appreciation.

Reflect on the Moment: Share a favorite moment from the party or express how much it meant to have them there. This personal reflection can deepen connections with your guests.

Choose Your Medium

Handwritten vs. Digital: While handwritten notes offer a personal touch and are cherished by many, digital thank you messages can also be thoughtful, especially if they include personal photos from the event or a video message.

Stationery and Design: If opting for handwritten notes, choose stationery that reflects the party's theme or your personal style. For digital notes, select a design that complements the event's aesthetics.

Timing is Key

Promptness: Aim to send thank you notes within two to three weeks of the party. This timely gesture ensures the celebration is fresh in everyone's minds and conveys that their attendance and gifts were truly appreciated.

Content Tips

Keep It Concise but Meaningful: Each note doesn't need to be lengthy. A few sincere sentences can effectively convey your gratitude.

Include Everyone: For gifts from a group, send an individual note to each contributor if possible, acknowledging their collective effort.

Addressing the Envelope

Hand Address: If sending physical notes, hand address each envelope for a personal touch. Use titles and names as appropriate to show respect.

Digital Etiquette

Personalize Digital Messages: Avoid sending a generic mass email. Personalize digital thank you messages for each guest, even if it's within the body of an email or a direct message on social media.

Closing Thoughts

Express a Future Wish: Conclude your note with a forward-looking statement, such as looking forward to the next get-together or wishing them well until you can thank them in person.

Thank you notes are a timeless tradition that honors the generosity and presence of your guests. Whether you choose the classic handwritten note or a digital message, the effort to express your gratitude will always be appreciated and remembered.

Reflecting on the Celebration and Gathering Feedback

After the excitement of the birthday party has settled, taking the time to reflect on the celebration and gather feedback is invaluable. This process not only helps you appreciate the success and joy of the event but also provides insights for future planning. Here's a guide to effectively reflect on the celebration and engage your guests in sharing their experiences.

Personal Reflection

Journaling or Note-Taking: Write down your own observations and feelings about the party shortly after it concludes. Note what went well, what could be improved, and any particularly meaningful moments.

Review Photos and Videos: Go through the collected media from the event. Photos and videos often capture aspects you might have missed and can spark memories of moments worth noting.

Gathering Guest Feedback

Informal Conversations: In the days following the party, engage in casual conversations with guests. Ask about their favorite parts of the celebration and if there's anything they felt could enhance the experience.

Analyzing Feedback

Identify Themes: Look for common themes in the feedback. If multiple guests mention loving a particular aspect, it's a strength to replicate in the future. Conversely, if there are areas of improvement mentioned by several attendees, these are important to address.

Utilizing Feedback for Future Planning

Create an Action List: Based on feedback, compile a list of what to keep, stop, and start doing for future parties. This action list can serve as a reference for planning similar events.

Share Appreciation and Insights: If comfortable, share back with guests how their feedback will influence future celebrations. This transparency shows you value their input and are committed to making every gathering enjoyable for all.

Celebrating Successes

Acknowledge What Worked: Beyond logistics and specifics, reflect on the joy, connections, and celebrations of another year of life. These are the true measures of a successful birthday party.

Share Successes with Your Team: If you had help planning the party, make sure to celebrate your collective successes. Share positive feedback and express gratitude for their contributions.

Maintaining a Record

Keep a Party Planning Folder: Store your notes, feedback, and any planning materials in a dedicated folder, whether digital or physical. This becomes a valuable resource for planning future events and continuing to improve as a host.

Reflecting on the celebration and gathering feedback is a process that closes the loop on the event planning cycle. It offers a moment to appreciate the success of your efforts, learn from the experience, and pave the way for even more memorable celebrations in the future.

13

Conclusion

Celebrating milestones, whether they mark another year of life or significant achievements, is a deeply rooted tradition that transcends cultures and generations. These celebrations do more than just commemorate a date; they honor the journey, the growth, and the experiences that define us. As we wrap up this guide, it's important to emphasize not just the "how" of party planning but the "why" behind each meticulously chosen detail, each laugh shared, and every candle blown out.

Milestones are the bookmarks in the story of our lives, highlighting moments of joy, achievement, and transition. They remind us of our journey, encourage reflection, and inspire us to look forward to what's next. Celebrating these moments brings us together, strengthening bonds with those who share in our lives.

Every person is unique, and every celebration should be a reflection of that uniqueness. This guide has championed creativity and personalization not as mere suggestions but as core principles of memorable party planning. From selecting a theme that resonates with the guest of honor's personality to tailoring activities that entertain and engage all attendees, creativity, and personalization are what transform a standard gathering into an unforgettable experience.

In your party planning journey, let creativity be your guide. Think outside the box, challenge conventions, and tailor every detail to create an event that's as unique and special as the person you're celebrating. Personal touches not only add depth to the celebration but also create moments and memories that linger long after the party is over.

As we conclude this guide, we extend our heartfelt wishes for success in all your party planning endeavors. Whether you're planning a grand celebration or an intimate gathering, remember that the essence of any great party lies in its ability to bring joy, forge connections, and celebrate life's remarkable milestones.

May your parties be filled with laughter, warmed by the company of friends and family, and illuminated by the spark of creativity and personalization. Here's to creating beautiful memories, celebrating the milestones that matter, and embarking on a party-planning journey that brings as much joy to you as it does to those you're celebrating.

Cheers to your success and to many unforgettable celebrations ahead!

Thank you for picking up this book, hopefully, it brought you an amazing celebration with your loved ones. If this book helped you and you want to make sure it can do the same for others please scan this QR code and leave us a review! We are so thankful for you and your review!

Made in the USA
Middletown, DE
08 April 2025

73878568R00066